—⚬⚬⚬—

The Handbook for Happiness

by Randy Millman

Questions and Comments please contact the author at:

justaskrandy@mail.com

—⚬⚬⚬—

Foreword

Randy is one of my rare students who has digested the essence of my teachings and has applied in daily life. In this book he expresses his wisdom he attained in life by living with awareness.

He has been successful in his desired material and personal accomplishments. Spiritual life is not an escape of material responsibilities but transcending them. Randy has found contentment with his accomplishments and finds joy to serve others by sharing his wisdom by means of this book.

My teachings contain bitter truth which may be difficult to comprehend for laymen. Randy has expressed spiritual teachings in a simplified, creative and contemporary way which is easy for laymen to understand and apply. Each quote provides food for thought for the day.

Yogi Shanti Desai. Author of eleven books on yoga and meditation. www.yogishantidesai.com

To my Yoga teacher
Shanti Desai

I am in a state of sincere and utter gratitude to have found someone that I am able share my life with and not be judged, but instead guided in a positive uplifting direction.

Although these simple words do not give my feelings justice:

I want to say thank you, thank you so very much!

Love,
Randy

We must be what we seek.

★★

If you want to learn more about yourself ask someone that doesn't like you.

★★

Middle path most difficult.
"eat too little, eat too much"

If a guitar string is too loose, or too tight,

it will not play.

**

Children only know the moment.
Be like the child.

**

Everything alive wants to live.

Positive sayings help create positive outcomes.

✰✰

To be successful surround yourself with successful people: then listen, learn and work.

✰✰

A foundation is the key to building.

Your career is your life, make sure you enjoy it.

★★

If you can't afford it, don't buy it.

★★

You'll get there, just keep going, but enjoy the ride.

Energy leaks out through desire.

⭑⭑

The sun is always shining but may be behind a black cloud.

⭑⭑

*Life is for **enjoyment** not **chaos**.*

Know what you are thinking.

✭✭

Humility brings in the honey.

✭✭

You are worth an infinite amount of money.

Sometimes listening is more than doing.

**

Friendship is when you are needed, convenient or inconvenient.

**

The body and mind is a finely tuned engine, always use high test.

Controlling your senses heightens awareness.

✪✪

See it, picture it, do it.

✪✪

There is no learning without suffering.

─≈⊙≈─

When you suffer you learn.

★★

The universe is infinite and so are we.

★★

Personal suffering could occur if you give too much.

─≈⊙≈─

Forgive yourself, if you don't who will?

✯✯

You are already happy; remove the illusion of what you need.

✯✯

Sometimes the past hurts. You can run from it, or learn from it.

If you don't forgive yourself how can you move on?

✯✯

The lessons keep coming with or without the teacher.

✯✯

Stop hurting yourself, start loving yourself.

Life is for enjoyment.

✭✭

Quiet your mind so you can listen.

Quiet your mind for peace of mind.

Quiet your mind so you can learn.

If you live your dream, your dream will live.

✦✦

Energy follows thought.

✦✦

Move energy from your good side to your bad side.

Stop blaming. Try moving beyond the who, and the why.

★★

When straddling a fence, make a decision or you will get weak.

★★

Everything growing today is from the seeds of yesterday.

While in a debate consult a wiser person.

✦✦

*Some gamblers lose once and learn for a lifetime,
others need a lifetime of losing to learn.*

✦✦

*Time will be wasted when trying to get
something for nothing.*

*Peace is **internal** first.*

✯✯

Create a surplus, then give.

✯✯

You only get so much time use it wisely.

—⊷◯◯⊷—

Each person has 24 hours in their day

Some people are better with time.

Why?

**

Stop blaming, take responsibility, and move on.

**

We can't fix others, but we can fix ourselves.

—⊷◯◯⊷—

Running in circles produces stress. Slowing down, stopping and thinking, creates energy.

★★

A Slow steady climb, and you shall be on top.

★★

No one person has owned the world, so why not enjoy it?

If you're looking through the eyes of love you will have a loving outcome.

★★

Love yourself first.

★★

*Save someone drowning only if **you** can swim.*

If you save money you will always have some.

★★

If you want to get noticed – stand out.

★★

All problems are solvable.

If you can't solve the problem,

someone else can.

★★

Your dream counts too. It's your dream, do it.

You're living in someone's dream,

now try your own.

★★

Eat less, move more, miracle in motion.

★★

Do what you have to do, then do what you

want to do.

Every day is a new beginning.

★★

Do what you love and love will be in you.

★★

Do what you love and love will shine through you.

❧

Don't worry it will pass.

**

Eyes speak,

thoughts can be seen.

**

When touching feel through the heart.

❧

Looking good, feeling good, try eating good.

✭✭

The apple will always love the tree.

✭✭

Remove old glasses to see new things.

Love is the only thought, all thoughts should stem from love.

✫✫

You can't stand in the same water twice.

✫✫

This soon too will pass.

Build confidence, build ego.

✶✶

Independence is strength.

✶✶

It's good to get away, now go home and enjoy.

Go without, create abundance

★★

Open doors, open mind, open arms.

★★

Whether your and "old soul" or a " new soul", it's good to be a **flexible** soul.

If you share, you have more.

✮✮

Your God – My God – Best Friends

✮✮

Don't judge the teacher, focus on the lesson.

Wisdom is calming.

⋆⋆

Baby steps = Marathons

⋆⋆

Recycle – Replenish – Rebuild.

All life is equal.

★★

You're right where you need to be.

★★

Start from where you are.

Consistence – breaks all barriers

★★

Frugality creates wealth.

★★

No effort is ever wasted.

Flexibility is the key to youth.

★★

You're perfect as you are.

★★

Life is always in motion.

God loves you.

✫✫

Beautiful heart, beautiful smile.

✫✫

Dance – Smile – Enjoy

Good in, good out.

✭✭

Impress yourself, not the world.

✭✭

Breathe positive, think positive,
and do positive.

Forgive yourself, forgive your friends, forgive all.

★★

Hug yourself, hug a friend.

★★

Slow down – Breathe – Meditate

*It's the **doing** that **is** the enjoyment.*

★★

Charity begins at home.

★★

Expect nothing, receive everything.

What else is there,

but love.

★★

There's beauty in all colors,

all colors beautiful.

Give what you can, no more, no less.

⭐⭐

Where is God?

Where isn't God?

⭐⭐

Money is like a seed, it must be planted in order
for growth to occur.

You're living the dream,
only, if you're working the dream.

⋆⋆

No one can live your dream;
remember it's your dream.

If you are running late; slow down, think, calculate, reorganize and then go.

★★

Share the pain, receive the joy.

★★

If you keep pain it will stay, share the pain and watch it go away.

This is a good sign when you are dreaming
about your dream.

★★

Education is useful when applied.

★★

You have the **option** of control if you know
what you are doing and why.

Right now is a subtotal of yesterday.
Recreate for tomorrow.

**

Courage, optimism, and focus create dreams.

**

Anger needs fuel, like fire needs air.

We all know we live **at least** once; **at least**
we should enjoy it!

✶✶

All hot water heaters have a release valve;
where is yours and when can you use it?

✶✶

Laughter is a wonderful release, do it often.

Because of the lack of sharing we hold onto pain.

★★

When sharing your pain expect nothing from the receiver, it's the process that is healing.

★★

We all have the right to be happy.

So what is blocking it?

EXPECTATIONS

*The process for happiness is **elimination,** not **accumulations**.*

**

*Try to recognize the difference between the **thought** of fear and **real** fear.*

If you are following in your parents' footsteps

make sure you can see your own tracks.

★★

Never be in a hurry to get killed.

SLOW DOWN driving!

If we are just passing through, make sure you use EZ Pass.

★★

*We might **resemble** each of our parents but we are **not** them.*

★★

Sugar, eggs, milk, and smiles are inexpensive; please give your neighbors what they need.

The world is round.

Send love out, and it comes back to you.

⋆⋆

Garbage placement, views, and fence lines are trivial; please give your neighbors what they need.

Surround yourself with mentors,

friends, and family. What else is there?

✭✭

Mentors love teaching, that is their enjoyment.

✭✭

If a secret causes you pain, share it, you'll feel

better in time.

If any abuse occurred to you, forgive yourself,
it was not your fault.

⋆⋆

God's lessons speak in many shapes and forms.

⋆⋆

The more you share your pain, the lighter you
feel.

Forgive your family, friends and enemies; it's
you *that carries the burden.*

✮✮

When suffering from insomnia, use that energy.

✮✮

If you cannot forgive; stay away from the
negative, surround yourself with the positive.

Respect your inlaws; they only want what is best for their children.

★★

Energy is a gift, if there is a surplus, use it wisely.

★★

The saint lies within the sinner.

A peaceful mind needs quiet;
internal and external.

✦✦

Expect nothing, then peace of mind follows.

✦✦

After winning a gold medal you may feel
disappointed; remember the journey.

―⊷⊶―

Consider all your inspiring thoughts, they were
sent directly to you from your source.

★★

The active mind is God's workshop.

★★

An enemy is just a friend you do not fully
understand.

―⊷⊶―

For a peaceful party try mixing drinks, not politics or religion.

★★

We all get angry and make mistakes. Maturity can be expressed with four magic words, "I am truly sorry."

★★

Pain lessens when you share.

One of the many joys of wealth is sharing.

★★

When the student is ready the mentor will appear.

★★

If relations are strained with your neighbor, buy them a gift and watch your relationship rebuild.

It's natural to push the baby bird from the nest, not clip it's wings.

✴✴

Enabling a child only weakens them and prolongs the inevitable.

✴✴

Life moves fast, like a flash of lightning, create some enjoyment today.

If you want health to stay,

laugh the day away.

✦✦

When opportunity knocks, answer the door

with a smile on your face.

✦✦

Happy or miserable, both are easy to see.

Stay calm, stay focused,

and stay on track.

★★

Enjoy your life – it's your life.

★★

Keep going, your time will come.

★★

Change yourself, not the world.

Change your outlook and when you look out
you will see a change.

✦✦

Begin with love, end with love.

✦✦

Love is what we are.

*Your dreams are individual gifts
sent directly to you.*

✯✯

*If you were abused don't make it mean
anything.
EXAMPLE: "I was bad so I deserved it,
or I am no good."
Forgive yourself, you did nothing wrong.
Now move on.*

Sometimes a little taste of hell helps us appreciate heaven.

**

It's hard to appreciate heaven if you have never been to hell.

**

Forgiveness is possible through the bitter truth and understanding.

Before judgment, know the question and listen for the answer, with an open heart and an open mind.

★★

Work towards a larger spiritual house and a smaller physical home.

★★

99.9% of fears never become reality.

—⚬⚬⚬—

Change is always occurring; the key is to change
with it.

★★

For a comfortable fit
try wearing your own shoes.

★★

If you need a reason to be happy,
just make one up.

—⚬⚬⚬—

When looking for wealth, don't look down, think up.

★★

Our minds are incredibly flexible; if given a chance.

★★

*What you are doing is important to **you**. Also remember , what 6 billion others are doing is important to **them**.*

Don't give your children too much.

Don't deny them their struggle.

✯✯

School is a wonderful place for an education

and so is everywhere else.

✯✯

Education will be in school and out.

―⊸⧼∘⧽⊷―

Be grateful for the 10 things you have. Not the 300,000 things you don't.

★★

Who you were, who you are, and who you will become are three different people, Although, they may look similar.

★★

Overindulgence can create problems.

―⊸⧼∘⧽⊷―

—◌◌◌—

If you are doing something you don't enjoy doing, stop doing it.

Remember you are the one doing it.

**

Each day is your last; enjoy it like it is your first.

**

All Roses have thorns; try to focus on the rose.

—◌◌◌—

When opportunity is knocking answer the door quickly.

★★

The longer you wear someone else's shoes the more it hurts.

Courage, optimism and focus create dreams.

✭✭

God bless God

✭✭

Love is not perfect, but it is the perfect glue.

Lost may be a loved one, but love is never lost.

★★

When you can't enjoy what you are doing.
Accept what you are doing and then peace will
follow.

★★

If it has an engine it will give you trouble.

★★

When opportunity knocks you can answer the door or hide behind it.

★★

We are all looking to improve ourselves, knowingly or unknowingly.

If you are miserable you need a reason

If you are excited you need a reason.

If you are blissful, no reason necessary.

★★

*The world does not revolve around **us**,*

*but it might be wise to revolve **with***

the world.

When someone's negativity is directed towards you, deflect it with a positive shield.

✶✶

When surrounded by negativity, get up and move to positive surroundings

What you want and what God gives
could be two different things.
Acceptance is the key.

★★

Just because you may have an answer
doesn't mean it will fall on willing ears.

Randy Michael Millman was born in Philadelphia in 1961. The youngest of three boys, and a younger sister,the family spent there early years in North Philadelphia. At the age of 8 Randy and his family moved to the suburb of Cinnaminson and eventually moved to Southern New Jersey where he started his own jewelry business.

It was around 1990 when Randy was introduced to yoga and meditation. He has been faithfully practicing meditation, with Yogi Shanti Desai of Ocean City, ever since.

Randy currently resides in Southern New Jersey with his wife Diana and son Cyrus. He is an avid poetry and song writer and enjoys playing his guitar.

Made in the USA
Las Vegas, NV
10 February 2022